Henry Ward Beecher

An Hour with the American Hebrew

Henry Ward Beecher

An Hour with the American Hebrew

ISBN/EAN: 9783337136055

Printed in Europe, USA, Canada, Australia, Japan

Cover: Foto ©Lupo / pixelio.de

More available books at **www.hansebooks.com**

1779-1879.

‑CENTENNIAL COMMEMORATION‑

OF THE

RIDE OF GENERAL ISRAEL PUTNAM,

AT

GREENWICH, CONN.,

FEBRUARY 26, 1779.

OBSERVED FEBRUARY 22, 1879.

GREENWICH, CONN.
GREENWICH OBSERVER BOOK AND JOB PRINT,
1880.

OFFICERS:

A. FOSTER HIGGINS, President.

Vice-Presidents,

FRANK SHEPARD,	JOHN G. REYNÔLDS,
JOHN VOORHIS,	EDWARD WILKINSON,
THOMAS A. MEAD,	SOLOMON MEAD.

Secretaries,

R. JAY WALSH,	HAMILTON W. MABIE.

FREDERICK A. HUBBARD.

Treasurer,

FRANK SHEPARD.

Committee of Arrangements,

FRANK SHEPARD, Chairman,

HANFORD LOCKWOOD,	B. P. SMITH,
SOLOMON MEAD,	THOMAS RITCH,
REV. CHARLES R. TREAT,	H. W. R. HOYT,
L. P. HUBBARD,	BENJAMIN WRIGHT,

ISAAC L. MEAD.

Marshal,

EDWARD J. WRIGHT.

COMMITTEES.

Literary,

H. W. R. Hoyt,
Benjamin Wright,

Rev. Charles R. Treat,
Hamilton W. Mabie.

Philip W Holmes.

Music,

Isaac L. Mead,
H. M. Fitzgerald.

Charles N. Mead,
John H. Ray.

A. Edgar Brush.

On Guests,

L. P. Hubbard,
Benjamin Wright,

Prof. Wm. G. Peck,
H. W. R. Hoyt.

A. Foster Higgins.

Finance,

Edward Brush,
Hanford Lockwood,

Thomas Ritch,
Dr. F. N. Holly.

Solomon Mead,
Dr. James H. Brush.

Procession.

Edward J. Wright,

F. D. Knapp,

H. W R. Hoyt.

Collation.

Mrs. Thomas Ritch,

Mrs. George Taylor,

Miss Mary Talbot

Mrs. L. P. Hubbard,
Miss Amelia Mead,
Mrs. W. G. Peck,
Mrs. H. Lockwood,
Mrs. M. Cristy,
Miss Lucinda P. Mead,
Mrs. C. S. Churchill,
Miss Lilu Manvel,

Mrs. H. W. R. Hoyt,
Mrs. Thomas P. Hunt,
Mrs. Frank Shepard,
Miss Adelaide Banks,
Mrs. H. M. FitzGerald,
Mrs. George Selleck,
Mrs. J. Voorhis,
Miss Ella Voorhis.

Miss Josephine Lyon,
Mrs. J. E. Brush,
Mrs. Ophelia Long,
Mrs. Chas. Mead,
Mrs. Augustus Mead
Mrs. John Ray,
Mrs. S. G. White
Miss Julia Bell

Decoration.

H. H. Holly,

Rev. Charles R. Treat,

Philip W. Holmes.

Reception.

Joshua Peck,
Moses Cristy,
John Dayton,
Joseph G. Mead,
Brush Knapp,
Cornelius Mead,
Joseph B. Husted,
Whitman S. Mead,
George W Waterbury.

M. L. Mason,
S. M. Brush,
Henry Webb,
Daniel S. Mead, Jr.,
Dr. T. S. Pinneo,
Wm. J. Mead,
Zenas Peck,
Matthew Merritt,
Edward Mead,

A. A. Marks,
E. A. Knapp,
Lyman Mead,
George S. Ray,
H. H. McFarland,
Dr. Sylvester Mead,
Jabez Mead,
Willard H. Mead,
S. M. Mead.

Reporters.

Hamilton W. Mabie,
Frederick A. Hubbard,

R. Jay Walsh,
George E. Scofield.

M. Stuart Cann,
W. L. Ferris.

Ushers.

E. Belcher Mead,
Dr. E. N. Judd,
J. Arthur Pinneo.

William Peck,
Joseph F. Knapp,

Wm. R. Talbot,
Nelson B. Mead,

Publication.

Prof. Wm. G. Peck,
Solomon Mead,
Frederick A. Hubbard.

Edward J. Wright,
Dr. F. N. Holly,

R. Jay Walsh,
P. W. Holmes.

PROCEEDINGS OF THE DAY.

The procession having been formed on Putnam Avenue, below the Lenox House, moved at about noon in the following order:

Sheriff Aaron Sanford, and Deputy Sheriffs John Dayton and O. Bartram.

Wheeler & Wilson Band, of Bridgeport.

Grand Marshal Edward J. Wright.

Aids H. F. June, James L. Marshall, M. D. and J. V. Close, mounted.

Veterans of the Mexican War, Prof. Wm. G. Peck, Prof. J. H. VanAmaringe and Justice Philip N. Jackson.

Veterans of the War of the Rebellion, Wm. H. Bailey, Marshal.

Greenwich Light Guard, Co. F., Fourth Regiment, C. N. G. Capt. F. D. Knapp, commanding.

Putnam Phalanx, of Hartford, commanded by Major F. M. Brown, mounted, and Capts. Dowd and Case.

Distinguished Invited Guests in Carriages, accompanied by Members of the Reception Committee:

First Carriage.
A. Foster Higgins, Esq., President of the Day, with Hon. Gideon Hollister, Orator: Col. S. B. Sumner, Poet; and Col. H. W. R. Hoyt, Historian.

Second Carriage.
John Voorhis, Esq., Vice-President of the Day, with Gen. Joseph R. Hawley; Ex-Gov. Marshall Jewell; and State Treasurer, Hon. Talmadge Baker.

Third Carriage,

Frank Shepard, Esq., Vice-President of the Day, with Hon. W. H. Putnam,
of Brooklyn, Conn., great-grandson of Gen. Israel Putnam, and Member of the House of Representatives of Connecticut; Jedediah
Pendergrast Merritt, Esq., of St. Catherines, Canada, grandson of Thos. Merritt, the Tory, who chased Gen. Putnam to the brow of the Hill; and Hon. Oliver
Hoyt, of Stamford, Senator of the
Twelfth District, Con-
necticut.

Fourth Carriage,

Col. Vincent Colyer, of Darien; Hon. Dwight L. Williams, of Hartland;
Hon. R. H. Rowan, of Norwalk; and Hon. Lyman Mead, of
Greenwich, Members of the Connecticut House of
Representatives.

Fifth Carriage.

Edmund Wilkinson, Esq., Vice-President of the Day, with Hon. Wm. E.
Raymond, of New Canaan, Ex-State Treasurer; Lieut-Col. J.
N. Bacon, Second Regiment, C. N. G., and Ex-
Sheriff Geo. W. Lewis, of
Bridgeport.

Sixth Carriage,

Solomon Mead, Esq., Vice-President of the Day, with S. A. Hubbard, Esq.
and Capt. John C. Kinney, of the *Hartford Courant;* and
Hon. Benjamin Wright, of Greenwich, Member
of the House of Representatives.

Seventh Carriage,

L. P. Hubbard, Esq., of the Reception Committee; with Ex-Representative
Bacon, of Middletown; Rev. S. B. S. Bissell, of Norwalk; and
Rev. C. E. Glover, of New York.

Eighth Carriage,

Thomas Ritch, of the Reception Committee; with Charles A. Hawley, Esq.
President of the Stamford National Bank; Rev. Dr. Rogers, of
Stamford; and Rev. Matthew Hale Smith.

Ninth Carriage,

Matthew Merritt, Esq., of the Reception Committee; with John P. Hollister, Esq., of Litchfield; Henry W. Lyon, Esq., of Westport;
and Hamilton W. Mabie, Esq., President of the
Press Committee.

Tenth Carriage,

M. Stuart Cann, of the Press Committee; with Mr. Warren H. Burr, of the *Hartford Times,* Mr. N. A. Tanner; of the *New Haven Palladium;* and Mr. Wm. A. Countryman, of the *New Haven Register.*

Eleventh Carriage,

Mr. R. J. Walsh, of the Press Committee; with Hon. John D. Candee, of the *Bridgeport Standard;* and Mr. Robert E. Day, of the *New Haven Union.*

Twelfth Carriage,

Mr. George E. Scofield, of the Press Committee; with Mr. Frederick Penfield, of the *Hartford Evening Post* and the *Boston Globe;* Mr. Joseph Ells, of the *Norwalk Gazette;* Mr. Henry W. Vail, of the *Shore Line Times,* of New Haven; and Mr. Edward Z. Lewis, of the *New York Sun.*

Thirteenth Carriage,

Mr. Frederick A. Hubbard, of the Press Committee; with Mr. Lawrence A. Kane, of the *New York Times;* Mr. Wm. W. Gillespie, of the *Stamford Advocate;* Mr. M. H. Babcock, of the *New York World;* Mr. J. Meads Warren, of the *Stamford Herald;* and Mr. Wm. M. Keeler, of the *Greenwich Observer.*

Chief Engineer James W. Finley, and Assistants: of the Port Chester Fire Department.

Putnam Engine Company—W. S. Chapin, Foreman.

Putnam Hose Company—James H. Merritt, Foreman.

Judge of Probate, Town Clerk, Selectmen, and other Officers of the Town of Greenwich.

Warden and Burgesses of the Borough of Greenwich.

Citizens.

After passing along Putnam avenue, and around Putnam Hill, the procession returned to the Second Congregational Church. The assemblage having been called to order by A. Foster Higgins, Esq., President of the Day, prayer was offered by Rev Charles R. Treat. Mr. Higgins then made the following address of welcome:

Address of Welcome.

———— '

Friends and Fellow-Citizens, Ladies and Gentlemen :—

It is my pleasing duty to welcome you on this anniversary of the natal day of our great and revered Washington, which we desire fitly to commemorate, and also at the same time to embrace in our celebration a suitable recognition of this being the Centennial of the celebrated events particularly connected with this our State of Connecticut, and its gallant son, second only to the Father of his Country in position, and surpassed by none in noble, self-denying, self-sacrificing patriotism—Maj. Gen. Israel Putnam.

Before proceeding to our exercises, I hope you will pardon me if I say a word as to the spirit with which we should approach and participate in these proceedings.

Our Government has wisely ordered that certain days shall be set aside as holy days—days in which all secular pursuits are to be suspended, and the thoughts directed, as far as possible, to a definite object. These days are great with some momentous event of the past, and themselves force each its object upon our view and consideration. The one to-day is the birth of that great and good man, to whom in so great a degree we owe our national existence and life. It will be sufficiently interesting to rivet your attention, to listen to the story and incidents which in connection with him 'and 'our great General, the eloquent historian will weave into the web of his oration, and to the burning words of the poet, who will carry these topics into the transporting and elevating realms of fancy ; but these will all be but as a man observing his face in the glass, or the evanescent dews of the morning, unless each one of us shall endeavor to draw from these narratives and words the lessons they are calculated and intended to impress. They are the love of our country—the veneration and grateful remembrance of those noble beings who, Christlike, gave up their social welfare and individual comforts, and underwent toil, care and privation for us, our children and future generations ; and the earnest, heartfelt and intensified resolution that *we* will *forever* preserve and perpetuate in its purity, our sanctified inheritance of social, political and religious freedom. Alas, our days are too filled with low and grovelling pursuits! Let us for once—for this day at least lift up our hearts to loftier themes and purposes ; bind down our wandering thoughts to self-examination, and ask ourselves, are we doing our duty to our country ? and determine that at least this day we will be wholly *patriots*.

We learn from the records of those who then lived, that immediately succeeding the Declaration of Independence our loyal State displayed a new standard, one side of which, in letters of gold, was "An Appeal to Heaven ;" on the other, the armorial bearings of Connecticut, which, without supporters or crest, consisted of three vines, significant of Knowledge, Liberty and Religion, with the motto, *"Qui Transtulit Sustinet"*— "He who Transplanted, Sustains ;" thus indicating the confidence of our forefathers in the protection of heaven. This same trust in God was evinced by one and all during all these trying days. Let us now lift up our hearts to that same Divine Being who has so greatly enlarged to us the blessings of which He gave to them but the promise and anticipation.

Prayer.

Rev. C. R. Treat, the chaplain, then read from the Book of Exodus an appropriate portion of the Scriptures, and offered the following prayer :

Almighty and Everlasting God, Creator, Preserver and Governor of men, we give thanks to Thee, that, when Thou created man, Thou didst endow him with liberty ; that Thou didst plant in him the love of liberty ; and that, when unjustly deprived of liberty, Thou hast been ready with Thy gracious help that he might regain it. We give thanks to Thee that, in the course of human history, Thou hast been leading Thy children into larger and truer liberty, and that Thou hast been pleased to place us, the people of this favored land, upon the high plane of a free, enlightened, Christian civilization. We give thanks to Thee, especially at this time, that Thou didst inspire our fathers with such love of liberty, liberty of speech and action, and liberty of religious faith and worship, so that they were willing to suffer shame, exile and privation that these priceless privileges might be theirs. We thank Thee that Thou didst preserve them from the perils of the sea, the inclement season, and the sterile shore ; and that, in the latter time of trial to which our thoughts are turned to-day, Thou didst sustain those that then were dwelling here, in their acts of righteous remonstrance and rebellion, and grant that their cause should triumph. We bless Thee, O God, we magnify Thy great and holy name, for the share that Thou hast had in all these great transactions, and for the rich inheritance which Thou hast permitted to be bequeathed to us ; and while we honor him who was the hero in the event we celebrate to-day; while we honor all who were the heroes of that day and time, unto Thee we give the greater honor, as is Thy due.

And now, O God, we beseech Thee, as we gather here, let Thy blessings be upon us. Let nothing be said or done that shall be contrary to Thy holy will. Let the eyes of all be opened that we may see not only the human actors in the scenes of that distant day, but also discern the presence and the part that Thou were pleased to take. Let the hearts of all be filled with reverence, and love and gratitude for what Thou then didst do.

We beseech Thee, also, that Thou wilt help us to rightly value the great benefits we have received, and the great responsibilities that come with them, and as we recall the price with which our privileges were purchased, be ready to pay the price that shall be required of us that they may be preserved. As our fathers were faithful in their time of trial, so help us to be faithful when the time of trial comes to us, and, in peace or war, to shrink from no sacrifice that may save our nation's life or liberty. Grant, we beseech Thee, that this may be to us a holy hour, in which we may hear the heroes of the past appealing to us, in which this heroic spirit shall take possession of us and make us noble, high-minded men, like unto them. This we ask in the name of Thy beloved Son, our Savior, Jesus Christ. Amen.

HISTORICAL ADDRESS.

———·——·

Col. H. W. R. Hoyt, was then introduced and delivered the following Historical Address:

Mr. President, Ladies and Gentlemen :--

In a quiet graveyard in the town of Brooklyn, in this state, Israel Putnam has long rested from his labors. Through storm and sunshine, for nearly ninety years the worn and wearied body of the old hero has slept in its well-earned repose. Almost a century, filled with historic deeds, and brilliant with the annals of great events, has gone by, since he was gathered to his fathers, but his fame has not been lessened, and the halo that surrounds his name has become brighter with the lapse of time. To-day the state of his adoption, through her legislature and voluntary organizations, and adjoining states, through their representatives, have risen up to do honor to his memory. His fiery courage, his generous qualities, his patriotic zeal and his important services, have made him a most prominent figure among the heroes of those days in which, amid the thunder of cannon and the tread of contending armies, the foundations of a great nation were established. His nature and education had well-fitted him for leadership, in that time of turmoil and achievement. His experience in the French and Indian wars, and the estimation in which he was held by the authorities, had given him a high position in the military forces of the state ; and when at Cambridge in 1775, Washington assumed command of the revolutionary army, bringing with him the commissions of the four major generals, issued by the Continental Congress. Putnam's alone was delivered, in consequence of a want of con-

fidence in those upon whom the others were to have been con-
ferred. The incidents of his whole life are tinged with romance.
He was familiar with peril from his early youth, and had he
lived in the days of mythology, the popular fancy would have
invested him with all the attributes and endowments, which
were bestowed upon the ancient divinities.

The exploit of General Putnam, which we now commemorate,
occurred at a period of deep gloom and depression in the course
of the struggle for independence. The spirit of the colonists
was unconquerable ; the fires of their patriotism were un-
quenched, but their government was a rope of sand. There
seemed to be no power in the Continental Congress to enforce its
recommendations and resolutions, or to provide for the supplies
and payment of the troops. The value of the Continental is-
sues had become greatly depreciated. The masses of the people were enduring hardship and privation with patience and
resolution. Occasional discontent manifested itself, and mutter-
ings were heard among the soldiery, but their faith was unfalt-
ering ; their determination unflinching, and although without pay, and partially without food, they remained steadfast to
the good cause.

The headquarters of the army for that winter, were at Mid-
dlebrook, on the Raritan River, in New Jersey. The battle
line extended from the Delaware northerly along the Highlands
to West Point, and then turning eastward followed the Connecticut shore as far as Stonington. In the fall campaign, Savan-
nah had been captured by the enemy, and the province of
Georgia was under the dominion of the British. Above the
island of New York, and a portion of Long Island, floated the
banner of St. George, and foreign sentinels paced their beats
from the Hudson to the East River. The British General •Pig-
ot commanded in Rhode Island ; but with these exceptions,
the Atlantic coast was in the possession of the patriots. Sir
Henry Clinton held supreme command of the British forces,
and from his headquarters in New York city, caused frequent
predatory excursions to be made up the fertile valley of the

Bronx ; along the range of hills that forms the backbone of Westchester County, and from point to point along the shores of Long Island and Connecticut.

In 1778 General Putnam had been relieved from duty in the Highlands, and was afterwards assigned to the command of the forces in Connecticut. He had the two brigades of the Connecticut line, one brigade of New Hampshire troops, Col. Hazen's regiment of infantry, and one of the four regiments of cavalry commanded by Col. Sheldon. His headquarters were at Reading, in this county, about six miles southerly from Danbury. From this point he supervised the military operations in this State, and maintained connection with the Continental forces on the Hudson. Detachments were stationed at advantageous places, one of his most important outposts being located in this vicinity. The territory from Kingsbridge to Greenwich was known as the Debatable Ground, and for the people within its limits there was nothing but anxiety and danger. Living along the border of the disputed territory, the people of Greenwich were in a most deplorable condition. Many of her sons were in the military service. Of those who were at home, a large proportion were openly avowed Loyalists, and a third class, who were living under the protection of British permits, secretly gave information and furnished supplies to the enemy. It was a winter of unusual severity. With but few exceptions the people were weighed down by poverty. Cold and hunger were their daily companions, and the most rigid economy was scarcely sufficient to supply them with the scantiest means for supporting life. The depreciation of the Continental currency ; the severe taxation that had been resorted to to enable the State to pay the proportion of the public debt, and the expenses of the general government that had been assigned to her, and the uncertain tenure of life and property, had destroyed all enterprise and rendered business undertakings impossible. Men moved about in fear and trepidation. Their hiding-places were in the fields and woods. No one knew the moment when a bullet from a concealed enemy might strike him down. Families were divided against each other; social ties were disrupted; old friends and neighbors regarded each other with hatred and distrust.

The physical appearance of the town has been greatly changed. The stately mansions that now adorn the street along which Putnam rode in 1779, were then represented by the quaint dwellings of that early day, with gable ends and long, low-slanting roofs. Just beyond the foot of the precipice now known as Putnam Hill, then stood the residence of General Ebenezer Mead, who was a prominent member of the Committee of Safety, and a soldier in the Connecticut service. On the summit of the hill, north of the old Episcopal church, was the residence of Jabez Fitch. The church itself was a plain frame building without walls, with the rafters showing overhead ; and was so frail a structure that it was unable to withstand the force of the gale by which it was destroyed in 1821. The rear of the building stood a few feet from the brow of the hill. The main country road, as it was then called, led through the village to a point near the edge of the precipice, and then ran northerly for some three hundred feet. At the latter point it turned sharply to the south, and, hugging the side of the hill beneath the rocks that frowned above it, descended with a steep inclination to a point about eighty feet south of the present causeway. Then, bending again to the east it trended off in the direction of Stamford. Northerly and westerly of the church, across the point where the passage-way has since been blasted through the rocks, the ground was level and unbroken. South of the church edifice was the grave-yard, in which to-day are seen a few lonely and deserted relics of the past. From the rear of the church, across land now owned by Rev. B. M. Yarrington, a fence ran easterly down the hill along the southerly margin of the old road. Between the carriage path and the fence, rough and untrimmed stones had been placed from time to time, forming an irregular stairway up the hill. The face of the precipice was covered with a growth of bushes. Westerly from the summit of the hill, and opposite the present rectory of the Episcopal church, was the old tavern kept at that time by Israel Knapp. The original building is still in existence, and is owned by J. Frederick Holmes, the stone wing having been constructed since the period of which I now speak. Still further toward the village, stood an old house on the northwest corner of the present homestead of A. Foster Higgins, and on the lot now occupied by the Greenwich Academy, was the residence of Moses Husted. At this house the American guards were frequently quartered. Just easterly of the church in which we are now assembled, stood the house of Daniel Smith, which was burned by Tryon, and on the lot across the street opposite the old Town Hall, had been erected another building, the property of Jared Mead. His residence stood near the present homestead of Frederick Mead. Angell Husted 2nd, owned a house on the land now occupied by the Congregational cemetery. Between that building and this church edifice, the house of worship of the Second Congregational Society-- in dimensions thirty-five by fifty feet --had been standing since 1730. Captain John Hobby kept a public house on the property now owned by Professor William G. Peck. Clemence Hobby lived on the site of the Greenwich Savings Bank. Another house was situated on the ground now occupied by the Lenox House, and from that point to Rocky Neck, on the Sound, there was not a building in existence. Opposite the Lenox House was a building then kept as a tavern which is still standing, and is occupied by John H. Sniffen. On the property of Jacob T. Weed, stood another dwelling, and near the residence of Capt. J. G. Mead, was a dwelling house that has been destroyed within the past fifteen years. On the brow of the hill, on the ground now occupied by the homestead of Col. Thomas A. Mead, stood another house, then owned by Col. Richard Mead. In place of the magnificent row of trees that now line Putnam Avenue, there stood three ballwood trees, two of which still remain. One of them is on the ground of Col. Thomas A. Mead, the other stands in front of the residence of the late Peter Acker, and the third stood near the dividing line between the grounds of Luther P. Hubbard and Professor William G. Peck.

The 26th day of February, 1779, is memorable in the annals of Greenwich. Guided by the records and traditions that exist; by the statements of eye-witnesses that have been handed down from generation to generation, we are able to put forth our hands into the shadows of the past, and rescue from oblivion the true story of the incidents of that day that stirs the blood at the bare recital. As to a few minor details of Putnam's exploit there may be room for dispute, but the main fact is beyond question. The morning broke cold and dreary. A feeling of uneasiness and uncertain apprehension had gained a place in the community. Down toward the British lines there was a movement among the soldiery. Out of that region of silence and desolation that intervened, came the sound of marching battalions, and the clatter of squadrons of horsemen. Their purpose and destination were unknown, but to the people of Greenwich, accustomed to alarm, these signs were ominous of danger. The official records show that on the evening of February 25th, 1779, a marauding expedition started from Kingsbridge, commanded by Major General Tryon, the Tory governor of New York. His force consisted of about fifteen hundred men composed of British and Hessian troops, and two regiments of Tories. At New Rochelle they were met by a small body of Continental skirmishers, commanded by Captain Titus Watson, who had been sent forward to reconnoiter. This company at once retreated, but near Milton, in the town of Rye, was overtaken and attacked. Their force became divided. A number of them were killed. A portion of the company concealed themselves in the swamps, and the remainder made their escape along the highway to the Byram river, which they reached in time to destroy the bridge, before they were overtaken by their pursuers. Over the hills at full gallop rode Captain Watson and his companions, to give warning to the few troops then in Greenwich. Col. Holdridge, of Hartford County, was in command of the outpost. Gen. Putnam had arrived but a few days previous, to obtain information as to the military situation, and was then in the village. At this poin occurs the first discrepancy in the traditions of that day, but the prevailing current of authority seems to indicate that his quarters at that time were at the public house kept by Israel Knapp, which was known in later years as the Tracy place. The enemy reached Greenwich at about 9 o'clock on the morning of the 26th. The small body of Americans were posted across the road on the eminence south of the Congregational church. They had two small cannon without horses or drag-ropes. A portion of them were deployed as skirmishers on either flank. leaving but about sixty men to hold this position. A contest here would have been madness. They had no cavalry. The enemy outnumbered them ten to one. The guns were fired upon the advancing column, and then the order was given for retreat.

In the van of Tryon's forces rode Delancey's corps, composed of Tories from Westchester County, who had enrolled themselves beneath the royal banners, and were the most bitter and malignant enemies of the patriots. At the approach of this body, charging at a gallop, the few Continentals withdrew from the field, and Putnam started on his horse for Stamford to obtain reinforcements. Along the frozen highway ring the steel-shod hoofs of the Continental charger. Thundering on in swift pursuit, ride the enemy's dragoons. The unexpected prize is almost within their grasp, Every nerve is strained to its utmost tension. The rowels are driven deep into the flanks of their steeds. Their steel flashes in the sunlight ; their scabbards clank loudly in the frosty air. Each man, ambitious of the glory of being the captor of so distinguished an officer in the rebel service, leans forward in his saddle, as though to lessen the distance between himself and the flying horseman. Nearer and nearer to the old hero come the pursuers. Only a moment more and the mad chase will be ended, and the American general will be a prisoner in the hands of his enemies. But by this time, the brow of the hill is reached, and the bold rider, to whom fear is unknown, who in his life time has bearded the wild beasts of the forest in their den ; who, in the line of duty has faced grim death a hundred times with unquailing eye, spurs his horse right onward across the precipice, and amid a volley of bullets from his baffled pursuers, takes his leap into history.

Here again the local traditions do not entirely agree. There were eye witnesses to Putnam's ride, both among the citizens of Greenwich, and the troops under his command. All the traditions concur as to the spot at which he reached the foot of the hill, but the place at which he began his descent, and the precise course he took are involved in some obscurity. Our story is that leaving the highway, he turned slightly to his right, and passing closely by the northeast corner of the church, rode near or directly down the steps. The other story places his point of divergence from the highway about one hundred feet north of the church, gives him a southeast course, and makes him strike the steps about one-third of the distance from the foot of the hill. Both accounts are based on statements made originally by those who witnessed the occurrence, but which have been forgotten or misunderstood in the course of frequent repetition. One thing, however, is certain, whatever may have been his starting point, he performed a deed which the rough riders who followed him dared not emulate ; which is worthy of historic mention, and is a glorious exploit for commemoration.

It is not my purpose to describe the events of that day of terror in Greenwich. The British forces scattered through the town and spent the time in spoilation and debauchery. Insult and cruelty, robbery and murder, characterized their doings. The wanton destruction of provisions and property of every kind proved their hatred and malignity. A detachment went to the Mianus River and burned the salt works, a store, a schooner, and a sloop. At nightfall the order to return was given. Reinforcements had arrived, and the Americans followed the retreating enemy, blazing upon their flanks and rear, taking prisoners, recapturing the plunder they had stolen, and turning the invasion of the British into a substantial victory.

Thus, briefly, I have performed the duty that has been imposed upon me, which has been simply to narrate the local history and traditions, as they have reached us. The eloquent historian of Connecticut who is now to follow me will fitly protray the character of Putnam, and vividly describe the stormy period in which he lived and labored. In later days when the existence of the nation, whose foundations Putnam helped to lay, was endangered, the old spirit of the revolution was again aroused, and deeds were done by the sons of Connecticut that were worthy of their fathers. For the land of Putnam and his compatriots is to-day the land of Lyon, Foote and Sedgwick. It is the land of Hawley and of Terry ; it is the land from whose farms and homesteads went forth fifty-four thousand patriots whose names are unmentioned except upon the muster rolls, but without whose fidelity and valor Lyon and Sedgwick and Hawley and Terry would have been as nothing. It is the land that in these days, as in the days of the Revolution, spared not of her substance or her blood, but sent forth her bravest and noblest for the maintenance of Union and of Liberty. And in the days that are yet before us, if our fair inheritance shall again become endangered ; if Liberty or Law shall be again assailed, doubt not that her sons, inspired by the example of their fathers, will again place themselves in the front rank of the peril, and above their heads the tri-vined flag of Connecticut, and the starry banner of the Union, side by side, shall be the objects of their love, their fealty and devotion.

THE POEM.

At the conclusion of the Historical Address, Col. Samuel B. Sumner, of Bridgeport, read the following Poem:

I seem to hear the song I cannot sing:
I see the picture I despair to limn:
Coy melodies cajole the harp I bring:
The canvas glows not, and its hues are dim!

O for a spark of the Promethian fire!
The voice and phase most aptly to portray
The sentiments which every heart inspire,
The memories of this Centennial day!

Let words, however tame, become at least
As seed on welcome soil at random strown,
Which by responsive zeal may be increased,-
Each bud unfolding blossoms of its own.

What is our earth without its monuments?
The thoughts and actions that survive their day?
What is the past but the aligned events—
Receding mile-stones over life's highway?

Ever the generations touch and go:
Ever the river rolls its mighty tide:
Each drop is inconspicuous in its flow:
Crevasses on its banks alone abide.

What throngs are these that visit the old world?
Pilgrims throughout the elder hemisphere?
Why go they, but to witness there unfurled
The banners whose insignia are not here?

A nation's history is its estate.
Its record is its catalogue of men.
So tested only, is it base or great,
And worth or unworth the historic pen.

Not ours, perhaps, competingly, to stand
So soon beside the immemorial Past ;
But one brief century with trusting hand
Into the balances of Time we cast.

One century! Tell me, in every sphere, --
In peace, in war, in thought, in word, in deed,
May not Columbia challenge the strict seer,
And justly claim her honorable meed?

A hundred years! Within that breath of time :
On this new soil, may we not dare to say,
Some proud achievements and some thoughts sublime,
Have had their birth, and shall defy decay ?

O surely, if we read aright the pages
Impartial history hath wide outspread.
The last have added to preceding ages
Their righteous quotas of the deathless dead.

And o'er this vast and virgin territory,
Have risen and do yet appeal to rise,
The monuments of such abiding glory
As wakes the nations to a strange surprise.

A hundred years! Go back that space of time :
No enterprise woke here the solitude ;
No rail or wire made instant distant clime :
No palaces supplanted cabins rude.

All things along this new-discovered coast,
Were primitive as primitive could be :
Affairs were unconceived which now we boast.
And tell us, whoso can, O where were we?

A hundred years! A hundred years to come—
The forms here circumstant, resolved to clay—
Mayhap may spring from hearts and lips of some
The thoughts we feel. the words we speak to-day !

But tune the measure into themes the moments here command,
And note the memories that surround the spot where now we stand ;
The very spot, where school books tell, a century to-day,
Old PUTNAM did his bravest deed—and bravely ran away !

You understand the paradox : I seem to see him now
Array his doughty phalanx there, on Horseneck's cliffy brow.
I hear the saucy cannonade : " Now to the swamp," cries he,—
" Where hoof of horseman cannot come. Leave what betides to me !"

His men in safety, there he sits, his faithful steed astride,
Provoker of a hundred deaths ; Valor personified !
The man of three score earnest years, outlined on Horseneck's brow,
A living statue for all time ;—ah, yes : I see him now !

On in the flush of victory, dash forward Tyron's van,
With fifteen hundred stout dragoons, to capture one brave man !
The hero wheels ; one thought, one plunge, sheer to the vale beneath
" Great God !" shriek the astounded foe—" he leaps unto his death !"

Now thick and fast as leaden rain, the murderous bolts are sped ;
They vainly pierce the old cocked hat, but spare the tough old head ;
Sure-footed steed ; brave-hearted man ; together safe at last ;
Well done, tremendous deed ! thank God ! the crisis hour is past !

[A supercillious Johnny Bull - the story goes -one day
A visit paid to Horseneck Hill, the locus to survey.
He turned upon his heel and said, " For all that he espied,
He didn't see that 'PUTNAM's leap' was such a daring ride."

A Yankee heard the cool remark, and with a Yankee's wont,
To always have a ready word to answer an affront,
Inquired : " When Gin'ral PUTNAM rid deown that ere holler,
Of all your fifteen hundred men, why didn't some one foller ?"

Some late wool-gatherer, we note, has found his printer now,
And seeks in covert way to pluck a leaf from PUTNAM's brow.
Forgive the mention ; let him in his native lair remain,
With that fictitious wolf, by mythical ISRAEL PUTNAM slain.]

Arrived at Stamford, " PUT," calls out the home militia band.
So re-inforced, rejoins his own, and re-assumes command ;
And as a curious sequel, we behold the hero then
Pursuing Tyron in retreat, and capturing his men !

Brief story this ; brief page in all that chronicle of deeds,
Which linked with Putnam's name, the whole world wonders as it reads.
Here, there, and everywhere, the same intrepid warrior still—
Crown Point ; Ticonderoga ; Highlands ; Horseneck ; Bunker Hill !

Such were the men who fought in revolutionary days,
Whose glowing names must aye invoke the tribute of our praise.
Well know we, later times have shown their valor has descended.
Unroll the scroll ; enlarge the roll ; keep all the glories blended !

Oh, ours is wealth of noble graves ; but nobler there is none
Than that where Putnam's form was laid, when life's career was done.
Upon his monument are writ, in phrase nor false nor hollow,
Sufficing word : "He dared to lead where any dared to follow."

Who knows but that the pivot point of all the war was there,
When Putnam plucked the flower success from nettle of despair ?
Who knows but that the very deed all other deeds to crown,
Was here enacted, after all, in this historic town !

When LaFayette, as nation's guest, came hither, o'er the sea,
Once more to greet the land he helped to 'stablish and to free ;
Not unforgot, he sought this spot, and little girls, they say,
Strewed flowers before him, and he wept, and they all wept that day !

I tell you, men and women of this proud, this loyal town ;
With all its pride its highest claim to glory and renown,
Its simple plea for world-wide fame—gainsay it whoso will—
Is this, that Israel Putnam once dashed down yon rock-ribbed hill !

May I not linger to suggest, nay, almost to implore ;—
As everlasting sentinel on this conspicuous shore,
Equestrian statue of " Old Put," as we recall him now,
In granite and enduring bronze, place ye on Horseneck's brow !

Make broad the field of view, so every train that whizzes yonder,
Shall carry hence in patriot breasts a patriotism fonder ;
And with their errands to and fro, convey the grand old story,
And unto Putnam and to you ascribe the praise and glory !

THE ORATION.

The President then introduced the orator of the day, Hon. Gideon H. Hollister, of Litchfield, who delivered the following oration :

Friends and Fellow-Citizens, Ladies and Gentlemen :—

The day selected for this meeting presents two central figures for our contemplation of quite different outline, but offering some points of resemblance. The one is of that historical cast which idealists had for ages figured to themselves in poems, paintings and sculptures; but which had not before been wrought into a fleshly mold—a chevalier statesman whose ambition never outstripped his virtue, and who, without theories, was the embodiment of all that theorists had dreamed ; of nobility in thinking and feeling, of simplicity in planning and doing. The other is a type of the common people, eager, impetuous, working out the problems of life as if unconsciously, and by the impulsion of an invisble hand. As these two personages were designed to fill different spheres, and that no time might be wasted by them in adjusting themselves, their orbits were prescribed by nature. They were born to what they were to be. The one was stately, self-poised, formed to rule by self-ruling. The other thought and executed as if by one stroke, so that the very firstlings of his heart might be truly said to be the firstlings of his hand. Something of the pomp of English manorial life wrought itself into the fibre of the one ; the cheery fellowship and manly equality of rural toil, quickened the sympathies and solidified the manhood of the other. Neither of them was much indebted to book-culture. No academic groves, no cloistered arches sheltered their years of development ; no Castalian fountain slacked their thirst, no Arcadian visions exalted their young dreams. The employments of planting and surveying occupied the one ; the other held the plow, fought the wolf from his sheep fold, and felled the forest trees to make a clearing for his maize and rye. Both were unrivaled in athletic sports, both were strangers to fear and to falsehood, both in early life prepared themselves for the arena of manhood by the struggles of border warfare with savages untamable as the beasts of prey that prowled in the woods.

A detailed account of the campaigns of the French and Indian wars in which Putnam was so conspicuous, would lead us beyond the limits of this address. At the beginning of these wars he was thirty-seven years old, and without military experience. Yet such was the confidence reposed in him that he at once received a captain's commission in the provincial regiment under command of Gen. Lyman, and soon found his company filled with hardy young men who were eager to follow him. This company was so often detailed for special service that it finally passed under the name of Putnam's Rangers. He was very fond of this irregular mode of warfare, and his genius was well suited to it. The discipline of camp life was too confining for him. His fertile mind needed to work out its own plans, whether in reconnoitering, in cutting off supplies, in demolishing barracks and boats, in surprising and bringing in scouts, or hiding in woods and swamps, and out-laying detached portions of the enemy. The Indians were chiefly allied to the French. These wild creatures lurked in all secret places from Albany to the head waters of the St. Lawrence and the Mississippi. Like wolves they prowled along lake borders and river banks, and committed their depredations under cover of darkness. The approaches of a regular army were too slow to overtake them, too easily anticipated to surprise them. British discipline was wasted upon such antagonists. It was necessary to hunt them as they hunted white men ; to skulk, to hover on the skirts of woods, to haunt the defiles of mountains, to burn, to exterminate. Precedent went for nothing in this contest. It called for original sources always at command, sagacity, suspicion, sleeplessness, celerity of movement, silence, keenness of observation, disregard of personal comfort, and the utmost stretch of endurance. In all these requisites Putnam's faculties were whetted to the sharpness of instinct. He loved these desultory ways with a passion intensified by danger. Difficulties that discouraged other men stimulated him, temporary failure quickened him, success beckoned him on to other successes. In these enterprises he had a singular control over his men on account of his unselfishness, his courage, and his truthfulness. Whatever he said was taken for verity. It was in the campaign of 1755, which resulted in the fall of Baron Dieskau, that he saved the life of Captain Rogers, by an act of gallantry that was requited with disingenuousness and treachery.

The campaign of 1756, resulting in the disasters of Oswego and Fort George, added new laurels to Putnam ; and at the beginning of that of 1757, he was promoted to be a major. The incompetency of the British Generals Loudoun and Webb has rendered this campaign but too well known in our annals. Had the command been entrusted to Putnam, the fate of the garrison at Fort William Henry would have been different. The next year, under the administration of William Pitt, Loudoun was superseded by Abercrombie, whose blunders fill so many pages of the history of that year. The details of these several campaigns, from 1755 to 1761, and the particulars of that sad expedition against Havana, lie beyond our limits. The Count de Paris, in his keen analysis of the recent civil war in the United States, has devoted a large space to the old Colonial wars, regarding them as a school of preparation in which the people of both the Northern and Southern States received that peculiar training and martial bias which enabled them successfully to cope with England in the Revolutionary War, and which, during the succeeding century, confirmed certain soldierly habitudes exhibited by no other people. The genius of these wars had for four generations been working in the blood of a common race, with qualifying differences in the two sections of the republics, until it broke out at Manasses and in the Wilderness, and culminated in the surrender of Lee, at Richmond. A citizen soldiery made up of freeholders, bred to the arts of peace, whose culture had made them averse to war, and who had resorted to it voluntarily, not for national and personal aggrandizement, but for the protection of life and liberty, and the defense of their lands, who took up the sword and laid it by with equal zeal and conscientiousness--presented such a contrast to the mercenaries of Europe, that the difference could only be seen when it had been worked out in results. . This citizen soldiery, stretching along a few hundred miles of coast, hemmed in by the ocean on one side, and a wilderness on the other, equally boundless and even more unexplored, who had brought with them into a desert the laws and rights of Englishmen to apply to conditions untried at home, were to overturn the theories of princes and prove that it is not the bayonet but the men who wield them, that think. Years before the breaking out of the French wars, Major General Roger Wolcott, who commanded the forces of Connecticut at Louisbourg, had forecast the value of such troops, and the influence they would exert upon this continent. But without the discipline of the Colonial wars, even to such soldiers, the consummation of American Independence would have been an impossibility.

Of all the chiefs of this border warfare, I place Putnam foremost, not only on account of his fruitfulness in resources and the fervor of his temperament, but especially on account of his long experience in it, at an age when the lessons of life are indestructibly wrought into the fibres of the man.

At the close of the campaign of 1761, this farmer-soldier, who had fought side by side with Lord Howe, witnessed the blunders of Loudoun, the pompous stupidity of Abercrombie, who had contrasted the phlegm of the British regular with the mobility of the provincial, who knew alike the chivalry of the Frenchman, and the treachery of his Indian allies—had treasured up a store of experiences and thought out a multitude of propositions that only waited the test of opportunity for verification. That opportunity now came. On the 22nd of March, 1765, the Stamp Act passed the House of Commons, and on the 1st of November of that year, it went into operation in Connecticut. Then came the daring protest of the Rev. Stephen Johnson, of Lyme, backed up by that of the other clergy, the organization of the "Sons of Liberty," public meetings of citizens, and town meetings, all breathing defiance. The forced resignation of the stamp-master followed. The timid Governor Fitch was soon waited upon by Colonel Putnam as the deputy of the Sons of Liberty. "What shall I do if the stamped paper should be sent to me?" asked the Governor.

" Lock it up until we shall visit you again," answered Putnam.

" And what will you do then?"

" We shall expect you to give us the key."

" And what will you do afterwards?"

" Send it back again."

" But if I should refuse you admission?"

" Your house will be leveled with the dust in five minutes."

Here is our border soldier reaching out and clutching at the forbidden fruit of parliamentary enactments. He fought beside Lord Howe, and caught him in his arms when he fell, but the tears that he shed were for the man, not for the nobleman. He has taken the measure of Abercrombie, Webb, Loudoun. Familiarity has done its work ; and now he is ready to pluck Lord Grenville by the beard. The farmer's homestead is too remote from the throne to be overshadowed by it. The roof-tree casts an ampler shade. Then came the Boston Port Bill, non-importation agreements of men and women, cloth-bleaching and the age of universal homespun. The news of Lexington found Putnam at work on his farm. He paid a brief visit to Gov. Trumbull, and rode into Concord in eighteen hours.

The attempt to rob Putnam of the honor of originating and superintending the plan of the entrenchments on the heights commanding Charlestown, has been so well sustained by an organized corps of writers and speakers of acknowledged reputation, that it will take many years to put the matter in its true light. The contemporary evidence all tends to show that Putnam was the author of this measure, and urged it upon the Council of War and the Committees of Safety, in the face of the most discouraging opposition. Gen. Ward, the Commander in Chief of the American forces had under him about fifteen thousand men, and expected an attack would be made upon him at Cambridge. He opposed Putnam's plan, and was seconded by Warren, and by most of the officers of the army. Putnam pushed the measure with all his enthusiasm, and finally carried it. How he set about executing his plan, how he rode from the Neck to the camp, and from the camp to the Neck soliciting, expostulating, demanding both men and ammunition; how coldly he was received and how poorly he was sustained by the timid Commander ; his exposure of his person ; his omnipresence in every part of the field ; his superintendence of the cannon ; the orders that he gave ; and how he brought up the rear of the retreat,—was but too well known at that time to need confirmation. One quarter of the men kept by Ward in the camps as idle spectators of the battle, would have swept the assailants from the face of the earth. Even the regiment that Putnam had brought with him from Connecticut, would have changed the fate of the day.

Putnam was now no longer looked upon as a border chief. He was at once recognized in England and America as a military leader of an original type, bold in planning, daring in execution, careful in the details of organizing, supplying, managing a campaign ; skillful in handling troops, and, in the words of Washington, "capable of infusing his own industrious spirit into his men." From that time to the close of his life he shared the confidence and affection of his chief.

On the 26th of March, 1776, he was ordered to New York to assume the command there. His conduct at this post and in that series of disastrous battles and retreats which followed added day by day to his fame. This was the darkest era of the revolution, and through it all, Putnam was by the side of Washington. He was in the rear of the army when it crossed the Delaware, and formed its shattered fragments in solid columns on the other bank of the river. His defence of Philadelphia, his conduct at Princeton, his success in protecting the country from marauders, showed him equal to the most pressing emergencies.

His next post was at Peekskill, for the protection of Fort Montgomery; and the task of stretching a boom across the river, for the obstruction of British ships, was assigned to him. The fatigues and exposure attending this enterprise greatly impaired his constitution.

During his stay in the Highlands, he selected as a site for a military post, West Point, the seat of our Academy. In the winter of 1778, Putnam was stationed at Reading, in Fairfield County, with three brigades, composed of New Hampshire and Connecticut troops, Hazen's infantry and Sheldon's cavalry, to protect the towns on the coast, the magazines on Connecticut River, and, if necessary, to reinforce McDougall in the Highlands. He kept a strict watch over the whole of this border territory, the old stalking-ground of General Tryon, whose depredations were usually signalized by some wanton destruction of such property as he could not steal. As this bandit was advancing with a body of about fifteen hundred men, upon West Greenwich, which was one of Putnam's outposts, the General happened to be there in person, with a picket of only a hundred and fifty men, and two small field pieces. He took his stand on the brow of the hill by the Congregational church, not with any hope of making a permanent resistance, but simply to do what harm he could to the enemy, and then retire. This unexpected reception was very telling, and the dragoons, supported by infantry, made ready to charge upon him. Putnam ordered his men to take refuge in a neighboring swamp, while he put spurs to his horse, and rode down the main street at full gallop, hotly pursued by the enemy's cavalry, until he came to the summit of another hill, on the brow of which stood the Episcopal church. An irregular flight of about seventy stone steps helped the worshippers to climb and descend the steepest portion of the precipice. The remainder of it was very difficult even for persons on foot, and probably no one had ever thought of traversing it on horseback. Down this precipice and flight of stairs Putnam plunged, and succeeded in reaching the plain at its foot. No British officer dared to follow him. A volley from the astonished rangers and a bullet-hole in his hat did no harm to the intrepid old man, who rode on to Stamford, rallied the militia, and turned upon the marauders. They fled, leaving about fifty prisoners in his hands. During that winter Putnam hovered like an eagle upon the coast, swooping down upon this noisome fish hawk wherever he showed himself, and snatching his prey from his talons. It should be a theme of cherished pride with you who live in these favored towns, that, they were watched over in their infancy by this kindly, fatherly soldier, who devoted the ripest and latest hour of his public life to protect them from the rapacity of the invader.

This meagre outline of the events of Putnam's military career will be the more readily excused because you have here a historian of such acknowledged competency to deal with them.

The fame of Putnam has pervaded the continent. It has gone into the log huts of the prairies; it has descended into the shafts of Nevada; it flows in the gold-bearing streams of California, and in all languages into which the letters and dispatches of Washington have been translated, it lives and blooms a perennial flower.

It has often been asked how it is that with slight apparent difference between individuals in blood and culture, there should be so little uniformity in results. One man is pre-eminent while he lives, and after his death penetrates to remote ages, keeping among men a kind of earthly immortality, while myriads fall in the race of life, and drop into nameless graves.

I am inclined to think that Putnam's success in life, and his posthumous fame grew largely out of his spontaniety of thought and action ; or, in other words, that he committed his powers to the current of his temperament.

He never thought about himself or what would be the result to himself of saying or doing this or that, but yielded to the inspiration of God speaking through nature.

In this way his soul became akin to the physical forces, the lightning, the whirlwind, the cannon-bullet, going where they are sent by a Divine direction, under laws which man may formulate but cannot make. This unconsciousness of himself does not imply a want of perception of the condition of affairs. He knew that if the British were allowed to occupy Charlestown Heights while their men-of-war were floating in the waters of the Charles and Mystic, they could command the peninsula. He knew that the entrenchments must be made at once, if at all. He knew that a blow must be struck then or the undisciplined American army would fall to pieces of its own weight. Thus his mind was a mirror rendering pictures of objects presented to it. His own danger, or personal advantages would have been reflected in this mirror had he held them up to it. But it never occurred to him to look at them. He saw the embattled armies, the cause that had arrayed them against each other, and the mighty results hanging on the crisis. They filled this magic glass and left no room for his own image. This is exemplified in his directions to his son Daniel, a stripling of sixteen and the child of his old age, on setting out from Cambridge, "You will go to Mrs. Inman's to-night as usual. Stay there till to-morrow, and if they find it necessary to leave town you must go with them."

" You, dear father," said the keen-sighted boy, " may need my assistance more than Mrs. Inman ; pray let me go where you are going."

" No, no, Daniel, do as I bid you," said the hero with shaking voice and eyes running over with tears. "You can do little, my son, where I am going, and there will be enough to take care of me."

Of a piece with this was his remark to Warren, just arrived upon the battle ground.

"I am sorry to see you here. General Warren. I wish you had left the day to us, as I advised you. From appearances we shall have a sharp time of it."

Seventeen years before, he had said to Lord Howe, the brother of the chief who was now advancing against him : "My Lord, if I am killed, the loss of my life will be of little consequence, but the preservation of yours is of infinite importance to the army."

Another element of Putnam's greatness was his large-hearted humanity. During the battle in the woods, near Lake George, in 1758, the French left three hundred men dead and wounded upon the field. Putnam lingered there late into the evening to see after the suffering Frenchmen. He gathered the wounded into one place, covered them with blankets, gave them wine and other delicacies brought for the use of his own men, and personally tended them. One officer whom he had placed in an easy posture against a tree, could only grasp his protector's hand in silent gratitude. "Depend upon it, my brave soldier," said Putnam, "you shall be brought to the camp as soon as possible, and the same care shall be taken of you as if you were my brother." In the campaign of 1765, after the revolting massacre of the garrison of Fort William Henry, in violation of a flag of truce, when he visited the smoking ruins and saw the mutilated remains of hundreds of men, women and children, he turned from the sickening spectacle with unspeakable horror. This humanity of sentiment was reciprocated at Bunker Hill by Col. Abercrombie, commanding the British grenadiers. When he lay mortally wounded, he bethought himself of his old comrade in the French wars, and, with his dying breath, shouted out to his men, "If you take Putnam alive, don't hang him, for he's a brave fellow."

Entire preoccupation and concentration of mind was another marked trait of Putnam. You all remember the story of his bird-nesting exploit in boyhood. In venturing out too far upon a limb in the treetop, he broke his prop and was left hanging in the air. He ordered one of his mates to fire a bullet through the bough near the trunk, and let him drop to the ground. The wolf story exhibits the same characteristic. The ravager of the sheep-fold had been tracked to her den. Putnam resolved to go into the cave for her. His neighbors remonstrated in vain. He was wolf-hunting, and the only way to come by the wolf was to follow her into her lair. It never once occurred to him that anything else could be done but to kill her ; and the danger to himself, as it was no part of *that* enterprise, was not taken into the account. This preoccupation of mind went with him through life. It led him into the presence of Governor Fitch, who was not long in finding out that stamped paper could neither be sold nor deposited in Connecticut. It went with him through the border wars, it crossed the Delaware with him ; it was present with him at Princeton, New York, Philadelphia, in the Highlands ; and stayed with him to inspire that last daring act of his life, the anniversary of which, you this day celebrate with the thunders of cannon and peans of jubilation.

Sternness in the discharge of duty was another characteristic of him. In 1777, while stationed in the Highlands, spies were sent into his camp by General Tryon, with a view of taking him prisoner. One of them was caught, tried and sentenced to be hanged. Tryon wrote a threatening letter to Putnam, hoping to intimidate him and thus save the life of his emissary. The answer and result you know. In the words of Mr. Peabody, " Putnam's military reputation, high as it was, concealed no dark traits of personal character beneath its shadow."

Putnam's disposition was purely elementary. With all his bluffness he had that chivalry of the heart that women are so ready to detect under all exteriors, and know so well how to value. Everybody loved him and coveted, not only his good will, but his affection. His neighbors vied with one another in paying little acts of heart-homage to him ; his family almost worshipped him, and his soldiers were ready to die for him.

Washington understood him perfectly, and made due allowance for his idiosyncrasies. In a letter to McDougall he said : "I have ordered General Putnam to Peekskill ; you are well acquainted with the old gentleman's temper. He is active and disinterested and open to conviction ; and I therefore hope that by affording him the advice and assistance which your knowledge of the post enables you to do, you will be very happy in your command under him." In December, 1779, Putnam went home for a little visit, and had just set forth on his return to the army when he was disabled by a stroke of paralysis from which he never recovered. Truth compels me to say that, notwithstanding his excellent moral character in all other respects, he had been, during his military life, sadly given to profanity of speech. He was subject to sudden seizures of passion, and in these paroxysms too often forgot the injunction, " Let your yea be yea and your nay, nay, for whatsoever is more than this cometh of evil." This habit he wholly abjured in later years. President Dwight, of Yale College, who knew him well, gave his written testimony in these words : " In the decline of life he publicly professed the religion of the Gospel." The Rev. Dr. Whitney, his spiritual adviser, has left us the following record : "He was not ashamed of his religion; his house was a house of prayer. He freely disclosed the workings of his mind, his dependence on God through the Redeemer for pardon and his hope of a future happy existence." This reformation must have been real, for Putnam was too ingenuous to make pretences. Nor was it a delusive fire sublimated out of the humid atmosphere of temperament, but a vital conviction that grew stronger as life wore on toward its close.

With all these remarkable qualities and endearing traits of character and with such a record of public service, it is not strange that we come together on the centennial day of this exploit to do him honor ; nor is it strange that the venerable Phalanx which bears his name and draws its inspiration from him, should retain so much of his vitality and perpetuate itself from age to age.

Here Putnam's public career ends. He was not constantly

confined to his house. In the summer and in the mild autumn days, he could ride forth to see his flocks and herds upon the farm, and visit his neighbors. His mind was still unimpaired ; his wit had lost nothing of its vivacity. He was often visited by Trumbull, Parsons, Wadsworth, Humphreys, and other gentlemen of the army.

Nor did Washington lose sight of him, but found time in the press of public duties to write him many a word of consolation. In one of these letters he says. "The name of Putnam is not forgotten, nor will it be but with that stroke of time which shall obliterate from my mind the fatigues through which we have struggled for the preservation and establishment of the rights, liberties and independence of our country."

Thus, in retirement, did Putnam spend the last eleven years of his life ; the patriarch of his household, the oracle of his neighbors, many of whom had been out with him into so many hard-fought fields, and brought back each his own garland of honor. On the 17th of May, 1790, he was taken suddenly ill. From the first he neither expected nor desired to recover. He lingered only two days. Every one of the vast concourse that followed him to the grave on the 21st of May was a true mourner. The grenadiers of the 11th Regiment, the Independent Artillery, and the militia of the neighborhood, with due honor laid him down to rest, watering with their tears the green sod that he had defended, and the spring flowers that prefigured the perpetual blossoming of his renown. Washington and Putnam—the first and second in rank and service in the War of the American Revolution ; the architects who, with all their prescience "builded better than they knew." The smoke of battle has lifted and left visible in the clear sunlight, the banner of St. George and that of the Republic floating side by side ; emblems no longer of angry strife, but vying as evangelists in carrying the laws, the language, the letters of a co-ordinate kinship to the continents and isles of the sea. Wherever these may go, as one century passes over to another the cheery "All's well" of civilization, those two names shall be hailed as watchwords of liberty till time shall be no more.

THE BANQUET.

At the conclusion of the exercises at the church, the officers and invited guests proceeded to the Lenox House, where dinner was served. Toasts being in order, the president gave, "The Day We Celebrate," and called upon Gen. Joseph R. Hawley, who responded as follows :

GEN. HAWLEY'S REMARKS.

Mr. Chairman and Fellow Citizens:--

If I had known twenty-four hours before that I was to respond to this toast, I should have, after finishing my work at one o'clock this morning, spent the remainder of the night in reading the history of Putnam, and preparing myself for this occasion, as I was sincerely desirous to come and pay my tribute to his memory. I approve of such celebrations as opportunities for the cultivation of State and National patriotism. There is no State in the world, that has had for two hundred and forty years a history to be so proud of as ours. There never has been a State in which the principles of freedom have so uniformly prevailed. You cannot find a country in the world, nor a State in this Union that can thus boast. I honor Massachusetts, but Massachusetts has no boast, except in the matter of population, which we cannot equal. The world cannot show a State or nation which has been so truly free, democratic, uniform, steady and conservative as Connecticut during its two hundred and forty years. It began with articles of association constituting a democratic government. The

charter of King Charles served as a free constitution from 1662
to 1818. Our allegiance to the monarchy was not prominent.
We chose our governors and all other officers, and swore them
to execute our laws. No king sent orders to our troops, or
levied them, save through our governor. We never failed to
furnish all troops required, cheerfully assuming heavy burdens
of taxation, and furnished more troops for the Revolution than
any other State in proportion. We had the only governor who
led his State into the contest - Washington's "Brother Jonathan"
– and furnished Putnam, Wooster, Hale, Talmadge, and a host
of good officers. In any field of intellectual, moral, educational,
inventive activity, our list of leaders is large. Reproached for
devotion to material interests, Connecticut has supplied men for
the most daring and chivalrous enterprises, both in peace or
war. Our legislation was always as liberal as any of its time.
Our schools should use a brief, clear, compact history of our State
and a copy of our constitution, well explained, as a text book,
that the children may grow up with respect for their State, the
more especially as so many of our people are of foreign birth,
or the children of foreigners. All honor is due to the orator of
the day, Mr. Hollister, for what he has done to place before
the people a history of Connecticut, and Dr. J. Hammond
Trumbull, who has made the history of his State an especial
study through life.

"The State of Connecticut," was announced, and Hon. Marshall Jewell called upon to respond.

HON. MARSHALL JEWELL'S ADDRESS.

Ladies and Gentlemen : –

"Connecticut!" This loyal old Commonwealth certainly
needs no eulogy from me; at least under these peculiar circumstances I could not give a proper one if I would, and if I
could and would, the lateness of the hour is a very good reason why I should not undertake it. Yet there are a few things
about the State that should make every citizen proud, in any
nation, and at any time, and they have been alluded to in fit-

ting terms. It has been said that we allow other States to take the lead, yet my experiences, wherever I have been, on this or any other continent, has been that wherever American enterprise and loyalty and prominence have been celebrated, Connecticut has had her full share of representatives. And so from our borders to the Pacific, wherever the sons and daughters of Connecticut are found, they are in the front rank giving a good report of themselves. I know that we are apt to say that these are somewhat degenerate days ; that the old days were better, and we allude to the men of the past as being rather superior, perhaps, to those of the present day. I quite agree with the gentlemen who preceded me, that ours are up to any standard. The men of Connecticut were strong in the early time, but in a later war, in a war within our recollection, we had also a great patriot. I mean the sainted and lamented Buckingham. I say, that, if in the time of the revolutionary war we had patriots, so we had in the last war, when Putnam's gallantry was equaled by Sedgwick and Lyon, and living heroes whose names I need not mention. I have no doubt that Connecticut, in the future as in the past, will do her full share when duty calls ; that she will supply not only the men but the materials so necessary to the maintenance of armies through long, serious and arduous campaigns. The weather to-day is not very pleasant, and yet this winter is not so severe, it is not so rigorous, as that winter when the Commander-in-Chief called upon the Governor of Connecticut for provisions to feed the army at Valley Forge, and met with a quick response. So it will be forever, I have no doubt. Connecticut will respond promptly and loyally whenever demands are made upon her. In the future as in the past she will illustrate patriotism and illumine history. I have no doubt for myself that with free speech, free pulpit and free press, we shall, in the march of time, illustrate those splendid traits which made the record of revolutionary times luminous with great deeds. I have no doubt, either, that the virtues and the loyalty of our ancestors will be emulated by their successors, and that we shall show to the world that whatever have been the virtues of the past, we shall not only keep alive the memory of Trumbull and of Putnam, but bear our full share in making honorable the history of our nation.

ADDRESS OF MR. SOLOMON MEAD.

"Greenwich in the Revolution," was the toast to which Solomon Mead, Esq., responded :

On the 20th day of August, 1824, Put's Hill was crowded with people. A few of the noble men who participated in the struggle for independence were then still among us and were present on that memorable occasion. The people came together to honor these patriots of the Revolution and especially one who was to be present on that day, the true friend of our Country in the days of its weakness and peril, who, like Washington and Putnam, was first in war, first in peace and first in the hearts of the people— Gen. Lafayette. After some waiting, he reached the hill, escorted by a military guard of honor and met his companions in arms. Their greetings were of the most cordial and tender character, while the air was resonant with the roar of cannon, the ringing of bells, and the applause of the multitude. These Revolutionary worthies then, with uncovered heads, walked down the hill, passing under an elegant triumphal arch which was erected over the road excavated through the rock, and beautifully decorated by the ladies with appropriate mottoes, evergreens and flowers. At the close of this reception, Gen. Lafayette went on to Stamford, escorted by a local military company known as the "Light Horse Troop," commanded by officers, some of whom are still living among us.

The last of those who were in active life during the war of independence have long since passed away. But the names of such patriots as Abraham Mead, who was a captain in the War of the Revolution, and Isaac Lewis, D.D., who was a chaplain, also Richard Mead, Zaccheus Mead, Andrew Mead, Humphrey Denton, Job Lyon, and others, are worthy of honorable mention. With most of these men I was personally acquaint-

ed, and well do I remember many of their recitals of the transactions of those trying times. This town, being situated, as it
was, between the lines of the contending forces, probably suffer-
ed more than any other town in the State. Law afforded no
protection for life or property. Some fled with their families
to distant towns for safety, some remained to protect their
homes as best they could ; others, possessing no high degree of
patriotism, resorted to the expedient of "buying their peace,"
as it was then termed, paying the Tories a stipulated price, on
condition that they might remain in their homes unmolested in
person and property ; while others, devoid of patriotism and
tempted by the love of British gold, gave aid and comfort to the
enemy by robbing and pillaging. To accomplish their purposes
they even entered the homes of their neighbors and stripped
them of their contents, drove off their cattle and live stock, and
whoever opposed them in this work did it at the peril of their
lives. Families were under the necessity of burying their provisions in the ground, or of secreting them in some other way,
and of leaving their grain in the straw, unthreshed, for years,
using only as immediate necessity required. Many worthy citizens were murdered by these Tories, others were taken prisoners, and driven like cattle to New York city, where they were
incarcerated, in the "Old Sugar House," a prison notorious in
history on account of the sufferings experienced by its inmates
and the great number of deaths that occurred within its walls.
Such were the dangers that some of our people, at the approach of darkness, would leave their houses and resort to
some secret place in the fields or woods, and there spend the
night. Still amid these trying times, a majority of the two thousand people, or nearly that number, who then were the inhabitants of the town, either openly or at heart, were true to the
cause of independence. And the fact is an impressive one, that
the frowns of Providence with very marked significance followed these Tories in after life, and to-day but very few of their
descendants are to be found. At the close of these eight years
in which such devastation and ruin ravaged the town, but little
remained but the bare earth.

It must have taken a quarter of a century to restore the improvements and prosperity that existed before the war. Could those who submitted to toil, privation, and even death, to lay the foundation of our prosperity, return to-day, with what surprise and delight would they witness the change that has taken place since those dark days! Truly, they would not know the place but from the few remaining landmarks like Put's Hill, Long Island, and the beautiful Sound that lies between. If in the past one hundred years such great changes have taken place, who of us, to-day, is able to predict the changes and improvements that would greet our sight if we might be permitted to return to this spot one hundred years hence? Who can say but that we might find our dwellings, public buildings and other superstructures of the most solid and most durable material, as slate, concrete, brick, granite and iron; our already commodious harbor sufficiently deepened to float our largest vessels, with ample wharves lining the shore from its point to its head; the roads of the town macadamized; numerous railroads running in different directions; our rivers dotted with numerous manufactories ; our village become "a beautiful city, set on a hill, whose light could not be hid," clasping friendly hands with the great city of New York across the Byram River. But great as these material changes might be, who can say but that far greater and vastly more important changes might be witnessd in the condition of the political, moral and religious world. Who can say but that the bright and long hoped for period shall have then come when truth, righteousness and peace shall have overspread the whole earth, and caused the rancor and turmoil of the centuries to disappear through the ameliorating power and influence of truth and benevolence, elevating man to a position much nearer his primeval state in honor, dignity and happiness?

ADDRESS OF MR. LUTHER P. HUBBARD.

Mr. Luther P. Hubbard replied to the toast "New England" as follows :—

Mr. President :

I am not a native of Greenwich, but for twenty years have been one of its citizens. I am a lineal descendant of George Hubbard, one of the first settlers of Connecticut at Wethersfield in 1634. He was a man of note in the colony, a member of the first General Court, occupying that position several consecutive years. Under these circumstances I feel at home here, for it is the sacred soil of New England.

You have given me a very broad subject for a five minute speech. I presume I was selected to respond to this toast because I have so long been connected with the New England Society in the city of New York, whose proverbial modesty never permits them to say anything good of themselves. And yet how much they might say! Stand on Plymouth Rock as I have done, and you will feel that the landing of the Pilgrims was truly one of the most sublime events in the history of the world. They came not for conquest, but to establish civil and religious liberty, and their principles have permeated nearly every portion of the republic. From that little band has sprung a nation of forty millions, with its orators, statesmen and poets among whom are Webster, Everett, Choate, Bryant and Longfellow, men that would be an honor to any country.

Lexington, Concord and Bunker Hill, tell the story of the patriotism and valor of the revolution, just as the schools, colleges and academies indicate the high educational character of the community.

Look at the Clergy of New England. Let them be honored and revered. They have always been self-denying and energetic, and the influence of those old divines is felt to this day. In the olden time one of the conditions of incorporating a New England town, was that "they should settle a learned and orthodox minister of good conversation, and make effectual provision for his comfortable and honorable support." The sentiment that made such a requirement was a mighty influence, and New Englanders who go to other places, go with the feeling that they have a mission to perform, and that is, to do good - to implant the principles of the Pilgrim Fathers.

As a type of the early New England towns, I will mention
Hollis, N. H., which with only 1036 inhabitants, has educated
and sent out forty ministers of the Gospel, besides numerous
literary men, among whom was Joseph E. Worcester, the lexi-
cographer. How they accomplished this is a wonder to us of
the present day, for I well remember when there was neither
carpet or piano in the town, and yet some of those sturdy farm-
ers had two or three sons in College. Many other New England towns have doubtless done equally well.

There is no portion of our country from which emanates such
a wide-spread moral influence as from the happy homes of New
England.

REMARKS OF MR. W. S. PUTNAM.

The next toast was greeted with tumultuous applause from
the humorous reply that Wm. S. Putnam gave to "Old Put :
His descendants worthy of their sire :" " I did not come here
to speak, I came here to see and be seen ; you must take the
will for the deed." At the conclusion of this toast the President of the day called for three cheers for the descendant of
" Old Put," which were given with hearty good will.

ADDRESS OF REV. C. R. TREAT.

Rev. C. R. Treat spoke as follows to the toast, "The Clergy."

Mr. Chairman, Ladies and Gentlemen :---

I feel highly honored by the invitation, you have given me, to
address you upon this occasion, and most highly honored by
the place, into which you have put me. To be permitted to respond to such a toast as " The Clergy," at such a time as this,
is a privilege that one well may covet. For it is not the clergy
of the present day, worthy as they may be of honorable mention, to whom this toast refers. The clergy, whom we have now
in mind, are they, who, a hundred years ago, in this commonwealth and her sister colonies, eloquently and effectually appeal-
ed to the people, to whom they ministered, to rise in righteous

rebellion against the unjust and oppressive rule of the government of Great Britain.

The clergy of the thirteen colonies, as all who know will bear me witness, bore no unimportant part in the drama that was then enacted. They were among the first to appreciate the burdens, which the people had been made to bear, and the dangerous tendencies of the measures, by which their rights had been denied to them. They were among the first to realize that discussion persuasion, entreaty could accomplish nothing more, and that the appeal henceforth must be made to the God of Battles. In private, in public, they boldly spoke, and when the time for action came, wherever duty called, they counted no cost, flinched from no foe, shrank from no sacrifice, and faltered not even when the cause, which they considered holy, seemed destined for defeat.

I will not, however, take your time to speak in general eulogium upon the colonial clergy. Far more worthily than I can speak their praise, has it been spoken and sung by many an eloquent orator, many a gifted poet, in the hearing of the grateful generations. You know the story better than I can tell it, and your hearts have often felt the glow of grateful appreciation and affection toward these heroic, high-minded men. Let me, therefore, as seems best in keeping with this occasion, speak briefly to you concerning two of the clergymen of the Revolution, who, in their respective spheres, bore a conspicuous part in the stirring scenes of that eventful time, and who both are properly associated with the experience, through which the people of Greenwich at that period passed. One of these, I am sorry to say, was not numbered among the noble men, to whom I have just referred, but the other was worthy of the highest rank among them, because of the patriotic zeal, with which he promptly espoused the colonial cause, and the unflinching fidelity, with which he maintained it from the first blow to the last.

From the beginning of the Revolution to its close, the pastor of the church, within whose ancient territorial limits we are met

to-day, was the Rev. Jonathan Murdock. At the commence·
ment of the conflict, he was professedly in sympathy with
those, that rebelled against Great Britain's unjust exactions.
But, after a while, he began to be suspected of a secret leaning
toward the enemy's side. This suspicion became conviction,
and found frequent and emphatic expression on the part of
the patriotic portion of the people. Upon one occasion this
minister met with a rebuke as ingenious as it was unique. He
was making a pastoral call at the house of Theophilus Peck,
who resided in the part of Greenwich called " Peck's Land."
As the hour for the midday meal drew near, he was court-
eously asked to remain to dinner. This invitation he accept-
ed and, as he took his seat at the table, expected that, as
usual, he would be called upon to invoke the divine blessing.
Instead of this, however, he was surprised to see his host
reverently bow his head, and then, to his amazement, heard
the following words issue from the good man's lips; " O Lord,
we have a wolf in sheep's clothing amongst us ! Put a bridle
in his mouth, and a hook in his nose, and lead him back to
the place whence he came."

This incident would indicate a feeling of deep dissatisfaction
and distrust in the minds of the people toward their pastor.
Farther than some such expression as this, however, the people
did not go while the war continued. Too much else demanded
their attention. By the time that Mr. Murdock had openly de-
clared allegiance to the British cause, Tryon's raid was immi-
nent, other marauding parties had already vexed and dis-
tressed the people, and, from that time, the portion of Greenwich
within the limits of the Second, or West. Society, was left
wholly unprotected from the enemy's attacks. No patriot could
longer live in security here. The best that he could hope for
was that his wife and children would be permitted to remain
to guard their homes, and to gather from their fields such a
scanty return as their feeble and frequently interrupted labors
could procure. To a large extent even this was gradually
given up, and the patriots of Greenwich, with their families

and a few of their household goods, sought temporary homes
in other towns, where they could be protected against robbery
and rapine.

In this state of things, it was not unnatural that Mr. Murdock should be left to enjoy unmolested the fruits of his disloyal-
ty. But the day of reckoning came. After the war had closed,
and the loyal men of Greenwich were at liberty to return and
re-occupy their lands and dwellings, as soon as it was practica-
ble, they began to prepare for action in this direction. On the
12th day of July, 1784, "at a meeting of the Church of Christ,
in the West Society, holden at the house of Mr. Benjamin Peck,"
they voted, "to call the Association of the Western District, in
Fairfield County," to their assistance, and to appoint a committee, consisting of "Amos Mead and Benjamin Mead, Esqrs., to
lay all matters of difference and grievance before them." This
committee drew up a formal statement of their grounds of
complaint against Mr. Murdock. Among these, as bearing upon the question of his loyalty, they alleged :-

"That, although he early took the Oath of Fidelity to this
State, and, in the beginning of the late war, showed much zeal
in the American cause, in the pulpit, as well as elsewhere, yet
contrary to his said oath of Fidelity, in 1779, on or about the
10th day of July, he voluntarily went to a British officer, with
a flag, then at the house the late Seth Mead's, in this place,
and there acknowledged his political friendship to the British,
and that soon after he began to justify trade with the then enemies of this State, among the people in this place, and Incour-
aged it by his own example."

They alleged further : -

"In May, 1780, he was, with his own consent, taken by Del-
ancy's Core and paroled, only to come to their lines a prisoner
when called for, but under no restrain by his parole, as to his
preaching or prayer. Yet, after that, he totally neglected in
public to pray for Protection to us, Discretion to our Councils,
or Success to our arms, to the great Grievance of the people
here."

As the result of this plain statement of the facts, the Consoci-
ation consented to the severance of the tie between this people
and their pastor, and they were left at liberty to seek a success-
or, who should be of one mind with them, and who should be
competent to declare unto them the whole counsel of God.
Such a man they were permitted, in God's kind providence, to
find in the Rev. Isaac Lewis, a man who deserves special mention here, not only because of his great worth, but also because
he too had been a Connecticut pastor during the period of the
Revolution, and, after it was over, became the pastor of this
church. His record during that trying time, is as bright as that
of Mr. Murdock is dark. Although he might honorably have
remained in comfort at Wilton, discharging the duties of preach-
er and pastor to the people of his charge there, free from the
privations and perils of the war, yet he deemed it his duty, nay
his privilege, of which he was not willing to be deprived, to cast
in his lot with his fellow countrymen, who went forth to fight for
their Country and their God. As Chaplain in one of the Connecticut regiments he faithfully served, until his health became so
impaired that he was obliged to return to his quiet home in
Wilton, and resume his pastoral cares.

Thus occupied, he, with many more, was rudely roused by
the raid, which Governor Tryon led to Danbury, for the destruction of the military stores there collected. Indignant at the
audacity of this attack, incensed at the outrages which the
marauding party had committed, the war-like spirit rose and
ruled in the heart of Isaac Lewis. Unable now to be contented
with the part of spiritual guide and comforter, he seized a musket, and used it with marked effect against the foe. Nor did he
desist from the pursuit of the retreating enemy, until he had
followed them to the boats, upon the shore at Norwalk, by
which they were to be borne to the vessels that had brought
them thither upon their destructive errand, and which were
to bear them back to the city of New York. So intrepid was
Mr. Lewis, so forgetful of himself, so eager in his attack upon
the enemy, that he exposed himself to the broadsides of the

vessels, that were waiting for the troops, and one cannon ball missed him by so little, that it struck the earth upon which he stood, and covered him with the dirt that it displaced.

Such was the man, whom the loyal men of Greenwich chose for their new pastor. They could not better have shown their determination to have a pastor as true to their country's cause, as they had been themselves. They could not better illustrate the radical reaction, the issue of the transition, through which Greenwich had passed, than by the selection of this staunch and sturdy patriot to succeed the temporizing tory, Jonathan Murdock.

Yet, as I thus speak, I feel rebuked by the kind and charitable spirit, which stirs in our hearts to-day. Too remote from us are the scenes, toward which our eyes have been turned, for us to respond to the spirit of righteous wrath that fired our fathers' souls. Too many years have passed since the last blow was struck, and the fierce, relentless conflict ceased. In the time that has elapsed since the struggle for American Independence, the din of battle has died away, the smoke has lifted, the battle field, its combatants, the ends for which they were both contending, can all be clearly seen. We, who were victorious, can well afford to confess that many of those, who strove against us, were as honest in their convictions, as brave in being true to them, as were those who fought upon our side. We can well afford to extend a generous judgment to all that were in error, and to forgive them with as hearty and complete forgiveness as we could wish from them, or as we hope to receive from Almighty God. We little know the trials through which the patriots of that period passed. We little know how easy it was for Jonathan Murdock and the ninety-two men more, who, with him, from this Second Society alone, changed from the Colonial to the British side, to take the step they took. We little know how difficult it was for those, who stood faithful to the end, to maintain their course. We only know enough to lead us to look with lenient eye upon Mr. Murdock, and those whose faith, like his, failed them before the despaired of victory came, and to regard with the greater veneration and affection those, who, like grand old Isaac Lewis, found their faith equal to every demand that the darkest days and the most dreadful disasters, made upon it.

ADDRESS OF REV. GEORGE TAYLOR.

Rev. George Taylor spoke as follows to the toast, "The 22nd of February."

Ladies and Gentlemen :

I supposed that I was to reply to the toast—the day we celebrate ; however, there is not much difference between the day we celebrate and the 22nd of February. Gen. Hawley made the day we celebrate a text on which to found a speech. I am in the habit of doing so occasionally, and the people can easily discern the difference between the text and the sermon. The General gave us an exhaustive sermon on his text, and uttered one idea which serves me at this moment, that is, that it is important that our foreign born population should be instructed in the civil and political history of Connecticut.

I think that public celebrations commemorating historic events and historic characters, will do more to instruct the ignorant than any text books that can be made, for by these means attention and inquiry are excited, and a greater impression is made than by reading. The procession and military display, the beautiful oration, the glowing poem, the historic statement, the recital of Putnam's heroic deeds, and the tracing of the social and political history of Connecticut, which has passed before us to-day, are more instructive than any other methods that can be used.

The 22nd day of February brings before our minds another distinguished man, whose character is worthy of our remembrance. It is wise, for nations and peoples, to appoint certain days and methods to recall the names and historic deeds of those who have rendered great service to their country and the world, by their heroism and their genius. On this day the

American people celebrate the birth of George Washington, who is called the father of his country. This is a custom that expresses the genius of the nation.

England is justly proud of her Duke of Wellington, France of her Napoleon the Great, Switzerland of her William Tell, and other nations of their great men, and while these names are admired for their military prowess, Washington is renowned and admired in every civilized nation, not only for his military achievements, but also for his pure social character, unquestioned patriotism and entire devotion to the will of the people. It is well for us, therefore, to commemorate the heroism and virtues of our great men, that our young men may be inspired with the national spirit, and be led to imitate what is good and noble in the character of the fathers.

There are days of sadness as well as of joy. A lady called on me for a duplicate certificate of marriage. She said, "I married James Russel on such a day, and a sorry day it was for me." It was a sorry day for England when George Washington was born and married to the interest of this country, but a joyous day for the American people.

When I was stationed in the mountain region, in the state of New York, a little boy was a favorite in the family with which I lived. At the time of our late war he was a young man and felt he must serve his country by joining the army of the union; he was wounded in battle and injured for life. I visited the homestead after the war, and the father recounted to me the sufferings of his son, and with tears in his eyes, said : "We consented that he should go to the war as it was all we could do for our country, and in the fear of God we gave our boy to the service of the nation, and, if necessary, offered him as a sacrifice on the altar of the union of our country, and all the other children agree he shall have the homestead and farm as his own." Give us a yeomanry like this, that will freely and religiously suffer and sacrifice for their country's weal, and we need fear no convulsion within, or menacing foe without.

COL. VINCENT COLYER'S REMARKS.

To "The Legislature," Col. Vincent Colyer replied:

Ladies and Gentlemen:

I came here expecting to have a quiet, pleasant time, and was enjoying myself immensely until about an hour since, when my friend Mr. Wright put a slip of paper into my hand, informing me that I was to respond to the toast, "The Legislature." Then my misery set in. Well, I have had a good time, notwithstanding. Mr. Chairman, and gentlemen, and ladies (I wish there were more of the latter in the room), you give me as a toast, as my good friend has said, the Legislature. Well, I have come to the conclusion that that means about every gentleman in this room. We go up there in droves, but come back and retire into private life. Now, this Legislature, gentlemen, so far as I have seen it, I think, will give a good account of itself, if it has not already done so, if these two gentlemen (referring to Governors Jewell and Hawley,) will please excuse me. [Laughter.] In that little matter of the Senatorial election we did our very best. We were like the Irishman in the play, when his two sweethearts visited him together, who said: "How happy I could be with the one, were t'other fair charmer away." When we found that one of these gentlemen would not let the other be elected, we then did the best we could, and (aside) I am not sure but that we have got a better man than either of them. [Great laughter, in which both the ex-candidates heartily joined.] But there's a good time coming for our two inestimable friends. Now for the Legislature, gentlemen. After that first little scrimmage was over, then came the question about the currency. Well, Connecticut had already received the key-note she should strike during this campaign, that a " dollar Greenback should mean a dollar in coin," and the very first act of this Legislature was to stamp that as the language for Connecticut. Other little acts have come up before us. Should you ratify our action, you will have a session once in two years, and it is estimated, gentlemen, and fairly estimated,

too, I think, that it will save the state of Connecticut nearly
a quarter of a million dollars in indirect and direct expenses.
Now, other bills must, and will, come up before us, and I think
you will find that we will give a good account of ourselves. Another very great and serious question is this, simplifying our
judicial proceedings. Why, I bought a little island up here on
the shore, and when our Chairman spoke of the delightful con-
tentment he has found in this neighborhood, I thought of my
own case—that was the very name I gave to my little island. I
was very happy when I was there alone, but another New York-
er came up and bought the other half, and we have been at law
ever since. Everybody else that ever owned that island has
had a row with his neighbor. They *do* know here how to keep
up a lawsuit. Beginning, I found that when I paid for that little
piece of land I bought a lawsuit. My predecessor had a lawsuit with his neighbor. It was about a miserable little piece of
salt meadow, worth about ten dollars. It kept him two years
employed, and me four years more, and I lost the case. So,
you see, I have a personal interest in simplifying our judicial
procedure. It is sometimes said our legislators can be bought.
I don't believe that. I don't believe any such thing. We have
a question before us on the reduction of railroad fares and
freights, in which you are interested. As to whether the railroads rule the State of Connecticut or the Legislature has control of the railroads, I have no doubt as to how it will be set-
tled.

I will detain you no longer. I wish some of the legislators
were here to-day to properly respond to this toast. You have
given us a beautiful edifice to carry on our deliberations in. I belong to a profession that make it a rule, while the picture of a
brother is in progress, to criticise it as much as possible, but,
when it is finished, then we praise it up to the skies. Two
years ago, when the new Capitol was in course of construction,
I criticised it considerably, pointing out its defects in the hopes
that the legislature, of which I was then a member, would cor-
rect some of its faults, which at that time could have been easi-

ly remedied. But now that it is completed I shall only say that it is a beautiful building. Some may find fault they found fault with St. Peter's at Rome, the work of Michael Angelo, St. Paul's in London, by Christopher Wren, and with the new Houses of Parliament. So we can, justly too, find fault with this building, but we have the most beautiful building in Connecticut. You were taxed for it, paid for it, and have got it. We are there, and I do believe that the Legislature (myself excepted) will do honor to the State.

MR. J. P. MERRITT'S REMARKS.

"Oldtime Foes, Long Time Friends," was replied to by J. P. Merritt. Esq., of St. Catharine's, Canada, who is a grandson of the man who led the British troopers in pursuit of the hero of this anniversary, one hundred years ago.

Mr. Chairman, Ladies and Gentlemen:

From the lateness of the hour, I will not detain you long, especially as I am not proficient in public speaking. After the eloquent addresses already, it would not be just for me to do so.

I find it incumbent on me to reply to the speaker before the last, "that members of the loyal party in this neighborhood used to skulk in the wood and kidnap prominent Whigs, hauling them to noisome prisons, and and in some instances shot at them from the cover of the woods."

A statement similar to this is related in a book, now in my hand, connected with the name of Shubal Merritt, my grandfather's younger brother. I am doubly bound to deny that such an occurrence, as that related of Shubal, ever transpired.

Mr. Merritt Mead, the author, assured me, twenty-one years ago, that he had no authentic authority for the statement, and I believe that, if his lamented demise in the defence of this Government had not occurred, he would have corrected the statement, as he then promised me he would do. My grandfather, in this connection, has told me that once, at the head of an adequate force, he was within half an hour of capturing

General Washington himself, and that a certain deacon, whose name I cannot now remember, was the cause of their failure, by giving the General information. " I am glad," said he, " that we did not succeed, as I entertain a high regard for the memory of Washington and J consider him an honor to our country.

As I mentioned at rising, I will not detain you, but am thankful for the attention you afford me, and will now take my seat.

PROF. VAN AMARINGE'S REMARKS.

Prof. Van Amaringe, of Columbia College, after referring to the courtesy and cordiality with which Greenwich received her guests, replied " To Our Guests," as follows :

Ladies and Gentlemen :

I am unused to being called upon on occasions like the present. I cannot do better than to say that when I was called upon to reply to this toast, I was more surprised than the inhabitants of Greenwich were a century ago, and I feel more consternation now, sir. Connecticut has contributed much in ideas and men to advance the glory of this country, and it seems to me that the principles which moved her, and enabled her to accomplish all that she has accomplished, are symbolized in the men and qualities which we commemorate. The moving principle was loyalty, and the qualities were keenness of thought and decision of character, and these traits found no more illustrious example in the Revolution than the sturdy patriot whose gallant exploit we celebrate.

ADDRESS OF MATTHEW HALE SMITH.

" The Press," was responded to by the Rev. Matthew Hale Smith, of New York.

Well, Mr. President, I would like to have you render a reason to me, why you have notified all these other gentlemen and called me up without giving me any notice at all.

I believe myself better able to describe this scene than to have participated in it myself. We belong to the peculiar class of men who, unlike the animal, have the tale come from the head. I think the true way to educate our people to loyalty and patriotism, is, in the first place, as you have been told, to-day, to have a celebration like this. When you provide the substantial fare for the body and the mind, upon which we have been fed to-day, your young men will be patriots at once. I claim, in the second place, that you ought to educate our people to stand ready, at a moment's notice, to turn prominent citizens to soldiers. There will be [no preaching, there will be no school, there will be no agriculture, there will be no commerce, unless you have soldiers. The Pilgrims landed on Plymouth Rock, and brought the elements of demoralization with them. For, eighteen years after they landed, it became absolutely necessary to call out the citizen soldiery to enforce the laws. [Laughter and applause.] Oh, you did not know this? Then I am glad that I told you. The law and the rule they laid down was that the officer should come out of the corps. There was Sam. Adams, who, from a simple citizen became a leader. Said he,"If you don't hang together, every man will hang separately." Well, sir, in the state of New York at this hour, there are ten thousand men ready armed. There is the 7th Regiment, that has saved the State over, and over and over again, from rioting, yet it is going around, hat in hand, begging money to build an armory. I like to look on these men. We can make officers out of the men in the ranks. When I was in England I was invited to take dinner at Mr. Morley's house, and they said I was to make a speech there. They had been speaking of our civil war. They had expressed their astonishment at our success, and had asked me, "Where did you get your officers?" and I said to them, "We made such men when we wanted them. We took our principal officers out of the tan yard, and we have got more at soak." There were a thousand men as loyal as Putnam. There were a thousand men who sacrificed their lives for the cause. We were always a fighting people, and if this country ever goes down she will go down as did "Cumberland," in Hampton roads, our flags all flying, our guns shotted to the muzzle, their last volley to sound our requiem. That is the way we'll go down, if we go down. But we shan't go down. We are not enemies of England. I can say here, when I look to that country, I am proud of her. Boys, be soldiers! Be soldiers of God, soldiers of Christ; soldiers of humanity! And, if a time ever comes, when we have got to go into such a war as this again, let us take the spirit we have heard of to-day, let us take the motto " Peace and good will to men," and entwine it upon our banner. Let us take the banner of peace. That is the only banner in the world that should wave over our own. With the two entwined on a better banner than the world has ever seen, we will march to the conflict, and fight till the victory is ours!

LETTERS OF REGRET.

The following letters, among others, were received by the committee:

FROM PRESIDENT HAYES.

Executive Mansion,
Washington, February 11th, 1879.

Dear Sir:— I am directed by the President to acknowledge the receipt of your favor of the 7th instant, and to say that he regrets that it will be impossible for him to attend the Centennial Commemoration of General Putnam's ride down Putnams Hill. He is therefore compelled to decline, with thanks, your kind invitation. Very truly yours,

W. K. ROGERS, Pres. Secretary.

Mr. L. P. Hubbard, Greenwich, Conn.

FROM MILES STANDISH, ESQ.

New York, February 12th, 1879.

L. P. Hubbard, Esq., Chairman Committee on Invitations:

Dear Sir: I am greatly obliged for the invitation to attend, on the 22d inst., the Centennial Celebration of Gen. Putnam's ride down Putnam Hill, and I regret that arrangements already made for that day will not admit of my accepting it.

If there is any single act of our Revolutionary War which, in this age of diluted patriotism and political self-assertion, is worthy of being commemorating, it is the act by which Putnam showed his forgetfulness of self in the necessities of his country. I am, sir, yours very truly,

MILES STANDISH.

FROM HON. G. H. PLATT.

WEST MERIDEN, Conn., February 19th, 1879.

L. P. Hubbard, Esq., Chairman Committee on Invitations, Etc., Greenwich, Conn.:

MY DEAR SIR:—I have delayed the acknowledgment of your invitation to attend the Centennial Celebration of Gen. Putnam's ride, in the hope that I might be able to notify you of my acceptance. But a pressure of business makes it impossible for me to attend. I regret it very much, for I feel that all such occasions are not only times of social enjoyment, but help us to remember, and stimulate us to imitate, the virtue and patriotism of those, who, in the early days, helped to make Connecticut what it is.

Very truly yours, G. H. PLATT.

FROM ETHAN ALLEN, ESQ.

NEW YORK, February 12th, 1879.

To L. P. Hubbard, Chairman, Etc.:

DEAR SIR:— I have received your kind invitation to attend the Centennial Celebration of Israel Putnam, on Saturday, February 22d, 1879. I regret that it will be impossible for me to accept your invitation, though, in declining, permit me to say, that, did circumstances favor, there is no one whose memory I would do more to honor than his whose patriotic fire enabled him to brave not only the tyrants of the palace, but the beasts of the field; whom neither the law of England, nor the wolves of Connecticut could subdue. Yours, very truly,

ETHAN ALLEN.

FROM CHARLES HOWARD WILLIAMS, ESQ.

NEW YORK, February 20th, 1879.

DEAR SIR:—I have delayed answering your kind invitation to attend the celebration of the Centennial of Putnam's ride, hoping to so arrange it that I could join in such event. Although a stranger to nearly all the citizens of Greenwich, I have been for years, as you, individually, happen to know, personally familiar with the location of the dashing act of "Old Put," and of the rich and varied beauty of the country around about; and I have, as though a long-time member of your community, the enthusiasm of the occasion. But engagements made prior to the receipt of your note, I am reluctantly forced to say, will prevent my attendance. In conveying my acknowledgments and regrets to those whom you represent, I beg to add that it has always seemed to me as not the least among the many noble favors nature and time have lavished upon the people of Greenwich, that the town has carried on her bosom the constant inspiration to acts of an heroic spirit. If what Longfellow tells us be true—and to send the truth of the poet home to every man, woman and child in Greenwich should be the one great purpose of the day, underlying and overtopping all its other felicities and pleasures—if it be true that

> " Lives of great men all remind us
> We can make our lives sublime."

then, who can go by the old lodge, at Putnams Hill, and not feel his soul quickened to a more exalted achievement of daily duty ?

If the day shall emphasize this idea in the minds of all who share in its festivities, it will have been a great day, indeed, for old Greenwich.

I have the honor to remain, very respectfully,

CHARLES HOWARD WILLIAMS.

L. P. Hubbard, Esq., Chairman, Etc.

FROM GOVERNOR ANDREWS.

EXECUTIVE DEPARTMENT, STATE OF CONNECTICUT, }
HARTFORD, February 13th, 1879. }

DEAR SIR:—Your communication of the 7th inst., inviting me to attend the Centennial Celebration of Gen. Israel Putnam's ride down Putnams Hill is received.

I regret that other and previous engagements will prevent me from being present.

I cannot, however, permit the occasion to pass without some expression of the honor in which I hold that impulsive and daring soldier, and my appreciation of the patriotic feeling which has impelled this tribute to his memory. It is eminently proper that those qualities of his mind and character which are exemplified in his prompt response, in the field, to his country's call, his resolute bravery at the wolf's den, and his reckless daring in the ride which you propose to celebrate, should be remembered with admiration and pride. And while such services as he gave to his country, both in war and peace, continue to be admired and imitated, we may feel certain that the safety and prosperity of our nation are assured.

I have the honor to be, your obedient servant,

CHARLES B. ANDREWS.

L. P. Hubbard, Esq., Chairman Committee on Invitations to the Celebration of Gen. Putnam's Ride.

FROM HENRY C. BOWEN, ESQ.

"THE ARLINGTON,")
WASHINGTON, D. C., February 20th, 1879.)

Mr. L. P. Hubbard, Chairman:

SIR:—Your very kind invitation to attend the celebration, on the 22d inst., reached me this A. M., having been remailed to me from my office in New York.

I most sincerely regret that my stay in Washington will prevent me from uniting with the good people of your section and elsewhere, in celebrating a most memorable event in our nation's history.

Of all the noble men of the Revolution, General Putnam stands to-day and will ever stand, among the very first, as a brilliant specimen of genuine American pluck and patriotism. In the dark days of our nation's history, he was worth a whole regiment of ordinary men. May the memory of his devotion and noble daring inspire us and all the people, with more loyalty and consecration to our beloved country.

If I were present at your celebration and were permitted the opportunity, I would offer the following sentiment:

GENERAL PUTNAM.—His sturdy patriotism, his self-sacrificing loyalty, his willingness to do anything, dare anything, and risk everything, for his country, should inspire all the millions who enjoy the fruits of his work with a sincere desire to be ready, in any emergency, to imitate his noble example.

With great respect, I am yours, etc., HENRY C. BOWEN.

FROM A. H. HOLLY, ESQ.

LAKEVILLE, February 21st, 1879

L. P Hubbard, Esq :

DEAR SIR:—Your kind invitation to attend the Centennial Celebration of General Putnam's ride, etc., reached me only last evening, in consequence of my absence from home.

A prior engagement precludes the possibility of my indulging in the pleasure of meeting yourself and the great company that will doubtless assemble on that interesting occasion.

In these times of questionable devotion to the best interests of the Union in some portions of our country, it is to be hoped that every citizen who may join that assemblage, to do honor to the memory of General Israel Putnam, may be imbued with the same spirit of patriotism and devotion to his whole country, which animated him in all his checkered life.

Desiring that all possible success may attend your gathering, I am very truly yours, etc., A. H. HOLLY.

FROM REV. LEONARD BACON.

New Haven, Conn., February 20th, 1879.

L. P. Hubbard, Esq.:

Dear Sir : —I thank you and the committee, very heartily, for inviting me to attend the Centennial Celebration of Gen. Putnam's famous ride.

I have been hoping that I might be able to accept the invitation, but I am disappointed. Other engagements are too imperative. I can only send you this inadequate expression of my regret, and my trust that the spirit of the old hero and those who fought under him may live in Connecticut through all coming ages. Respectfully yours,

LEONARD BACON.

FROM GEN. J. A. GARFIELD.

House of Representatives, }
Washington, D. C., February 11th, 1879. }

L. P. Hubbard, Esq., Greenwich, Conn.:

Dear Sir: Yours of the 8th inst., inviting me to attend the Putnam Centennial Celebration on the 22d inst., is received.

My duties here in the closing days of the session, render it impossible for me to accept. I regret that I am not able to join in this tribute to the memory of the sturdy old hero who contributed so nobly to the achievement of our independence. Very truly yours,

J. A. GARFIELD.

FROM REV. W. F. HATFIELD.

305 West 18th Street. New York, February 20th, 1879.

Mr L. P. Hubbard:

Dear Sir: —Please accept my thanks for the honor of your kind invitation to attend the Centennial Celebration of General Israel Putnam's ride down Putnam's Hill, on Saturday, February 22d. It would afford me great pleasure to be present on an occasion so fraught with interest to every American citizen, especially to those who are the descendants of the families of the Republic, and sons, or the adopted sons of your honored State, but a previous engagement will debar me from this privilege.

Trusting and believing that the ceremonies of the day will tend to strengthen the affection and veneration with which we cherish the memory of the heroes of the Revolution, and that all who participate in them will take a deeper interest in the welfare of our country.

I remain yours, very truly,

W. F. HATFIELD.

Loan Exhibition

OF REVOLUTIONARY RELICS, AT THE PUTNAM COTTAGE,
FEBRUARY 22, 1879.

———

Dr. Holly—Pair Brass Candlesticks, Copper Coal Scuttle.

Mrs. Jabez Mead—Pair Brass Candlesticks, Home-made Bed Quilt, Bible, 1769, Pewter Platter, 1769, Portrait General E. Mead, 1779, pair Wool Cards, 1772, Chair, 1769, Child's Jacket, 1769, pair Pockets, 1769, Picture of Putnam's Ride.

Mrs. Yarrington—Pair Andirons, Brass Fender.

Mrs. Jessup—Tea Pot, Sugar Bowl, Milk Pitcher.

Captain McKay—China Tea Pot, China Tea Caddy, two Tea Cups, two China Cake Plates, pair Wine Glasses, Tumbler.

Mark Banks—Washington's Beef Cutter, pair Knee Buckles, one Jeweled Shoe Buckle, Coffee Pot, Milk Pitcher, Slop Bowl, Tea Cup, all China, Wedgewood Tea Pot and Sugar Bowl.

Mrs. Yarrington—Snuffers and Tray, pair Bellows, pair Andirons.

Mrs. Alvin Mead—Old Arm Chair, 1779.

Mrs. W. R. Talbot—One Sofa Chair 200 years old, Chair came over with the Huguenots; one Set English China, thirty pieces, with Case; one Table, one Cover.

Mrs. Button—One pair Silver Candlesticks, Snuffers and Tray, one pair Cups and Saucers, one Wedgewood Vase.

Mrs. W. G. Peck—Two pair Bellows, 1776, one Swift, one pair Silvered Pottery Pitchers, Aaron Burr's Saucer, with Silver Sand, Feather Cape, one Toby, Tifa from Aaron Burr's House, Cup and Saucer, Silver Bible Clasp, Ancient Purse, with Continental Money, Spool Reel.

Mrs. J. Brush—Bed Quilt, Portrait of Lady, painted in 1758.

Mrs. Jessup—Picture of Putnam's Ride, Mortar and Pestle, Portrait of Mrs. Margaret McKay.

Mrs. Reynolds—Silk Shawl.

Mrs. Augustus Mead—Water Bottle, Revolutionary Musket.

Henry Webb—Pewter Platter, Bed Warmer.

Mrs. Treat—Pewter Platter.

Mrs. Churchill—Flag.

Mrs. W. B. Davis—Roger William' Chair.

E. Brush—Old Comb, found in the Putnam Cottage.

Mrs. Talbot—Brazier, 1779.

Abram Mead—Shoe Last, 129 years old, Butter Spaddle, 1776. Cane, 140 years old.

J. R. Lawrence—Samples.

Mrs. Jabez Mead—Sword.

Mrs. R——— —Large China Tea Pot, Silvered Pottery Tea Pot and Sugar Bowl, Tuscan China.

Mrs. Betts—Chair, 100 years old.

Mrs. Sniffin—Photograph.

Mrs. Jabez Mead—Chair, Reel, Spinning Wheel, Table Cover.

Mrs. T. Mason—Table.

Mrs. N. Bush—Old Arm Chair, 1781, brought from England to Mrs. Hannah Bush 1681.

Mrs. Nelson Bush—Portrait, painted about 1759, three Chairs, 150 years years old. Cannon Ball.

Mrs. Peck—Portrait of Captain Samuel Dayton.

Mrs. Titus Mead—Old Clock, two Chairs.

D. S. Mead—Chair, 200 years old, Revolutionary Musket, from Putnam Cottage, three Chairs, Cartridge Box.

Mrs. Yarrington—Chaffing Dish, China Vases, Colonial Money, Table, China Plate.

Miss McComb—Cup and Saucer, Silk Shawl.

Mrs. Edward Mead—Tripod Candlestick, Platter, Plate.

Mr. Wilkinson—Liquor Case, Chair.

Mrs. Peck—Table, Shawl, Glass, Cup and Saucer, Brass Fender.